God's Garden

A Story about What Happens When We Die

By Kevin Morrison

Illustrated by Patricia Bachoc

Ambassador
Children's Books
Mahwah • New Jersey

Library of Congress Cataloging-in-Publication Data

Morrison, Kevin, 1973-
  God's garden : a story about what happens when we die / written by
Kevin Morrison ; illustrated by Patricia Bachoc.
       p. cm.
   ISBN 978-0-8091-6741-8 (alk. paper)
   1. Death--Religious aspects--Christianity--Juvenile literature. I.
Bachoc, Patricia. II. Title.
  BT825.M66 2008
  236'.1--dc22
                                    2008038506
Published by Ambassador Books
An imprint of Paulist Press
997 Macarthur Boulevard
Mahwah, New Jersey 07430

www.ambassadorbooks.com

Printed and bound in China

In memory of Elinor Newman,
a beautiful flower in God's Garden.

— S.D.G.

As they had done many times, Danny and his parents walked to church. But today was different.
This time they were going to a funeral.

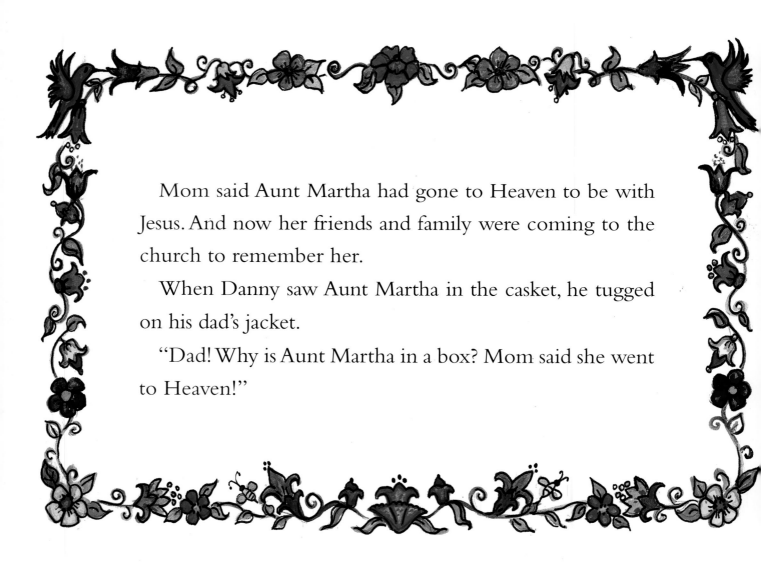

Mom said Aunt Martha had gone to Heaven to be with Jesus. And now her friends and family were coming to the church to remember her.

When Danny saw Aunt Martha in the casket, he tugged on his dad's jacket.

"Dad! Why is Aunt Martha in a box? Mom said she went to Heaven!"

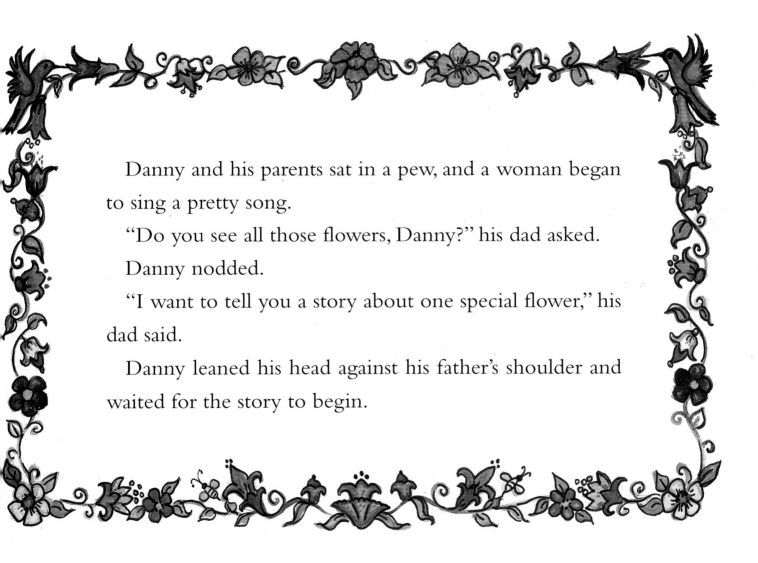

Danny and his parents sat in a pew, and a woman began to sing a pretty song.

"Do you see all those flowers, Danny?" his dad asked.

Danny nodded.

"I want to tell you a story about one special flower," his dad said.

Danny leaned his head against his father's shoulder and waited for the story to begin.

"Once there was a tiny, round seed. It didn't look like very much. But that seed was the spirit of a beautiful flower.

There was a Gardener who loved the seed and knew the perfect place for it. It was a place where the seed could grow into the most beautiful flower it could be.

The Gardener planted the seed in a sunny spot.
He watched it and smiled as he watched it grow.

Before long, the tiny seed became a little sprout, and then it grew into a lovely flower. The Gardener was happy.

All of the other flowers were happy, too. The bushes and even the bugs loved the flower.

The Gardener's plan had worked. That little seed had brought a special beauty to the garden.

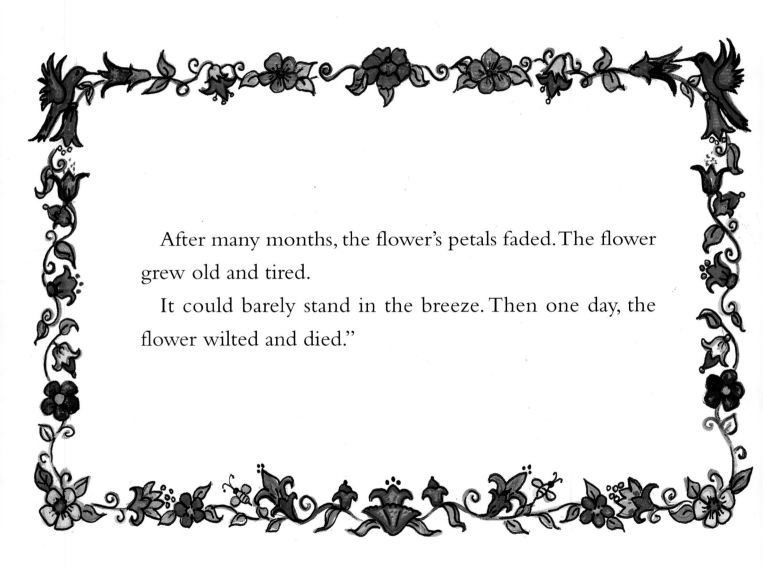

After many months, the flower's petals faded. The flower grew old and tired.

It could barely stand in the breeze. Then one day, the flower wilted and died."

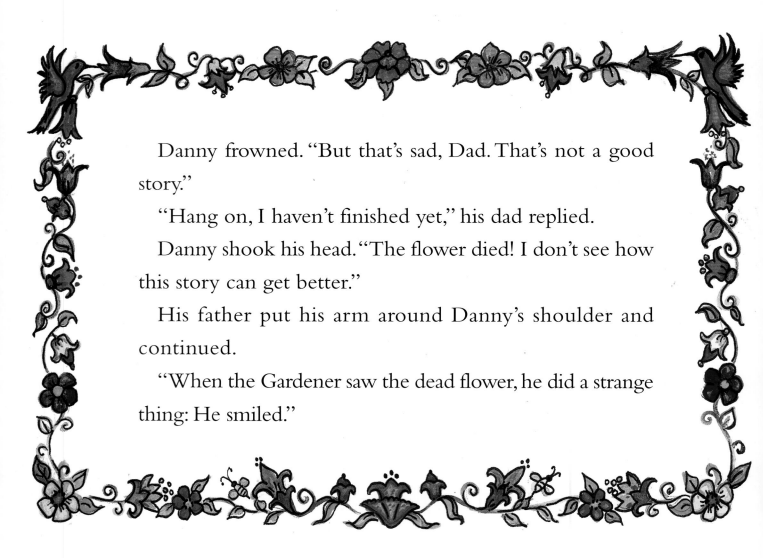

Danny frowned. "But that's sad, Dad. That's not a good story."

"Hang on, I haven't finished yet," his dad replied.

Danny shook his head. "The flower died! I don't see how this story can get better."

His father put his arm around Danny's shoulder and continued.

"When the Gardener saw the dead flower, he did a strange thing: He smiled."

19

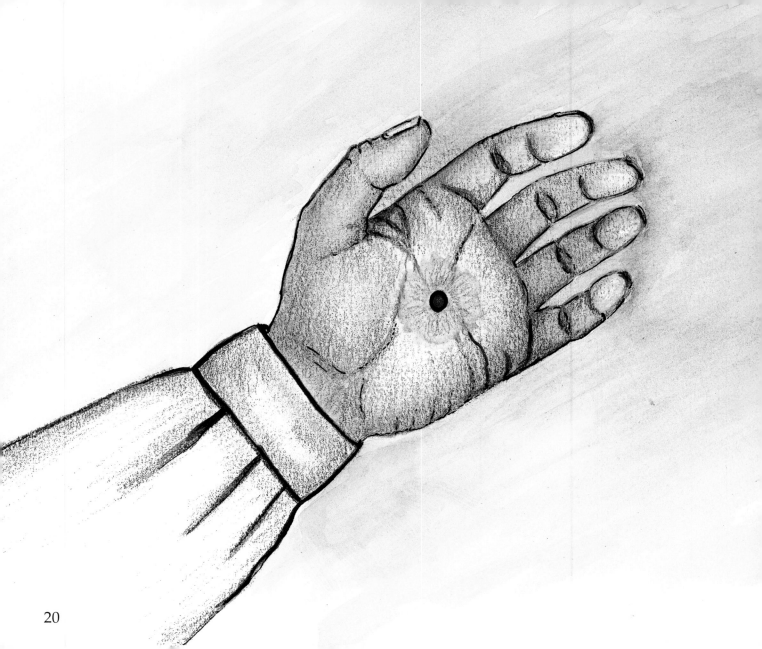

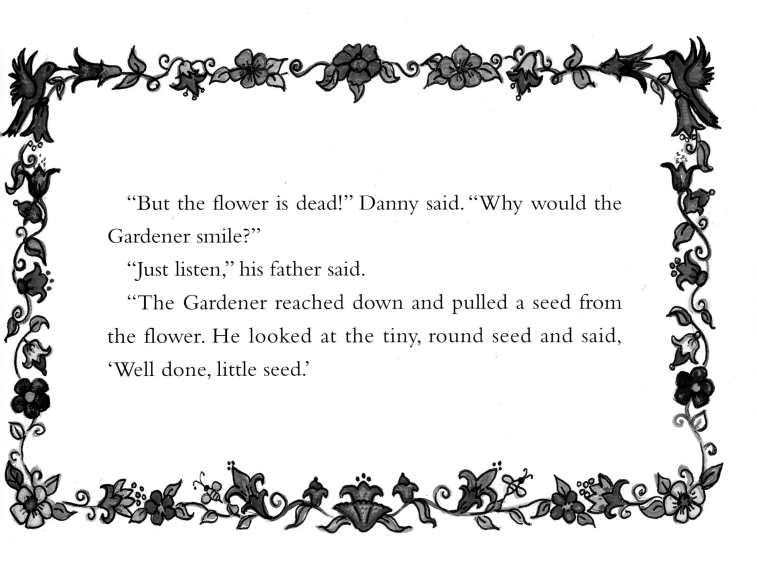

"But the flower is dead!" Danny said. "Why would the Gardener smile?"

"Just listen," his father said.

"The Gardener reached down and pulled a seed from the flower. He looked at the tiny, round seed and said, 'Well done, little seed.'

Then the Gardener took the seed to an amazing place.

It was more beautiful than any garden anybody has ever seen. It was filled with everything from moss to flowers to mighty oak trees.

The Gardener had a special
place saved for the seed in his beautiful
garden, and he replanted it.

23

Once again the seed became a flower. But this time it was more beautiful than before.

And in this garden, the flower lived forever. It would never die."

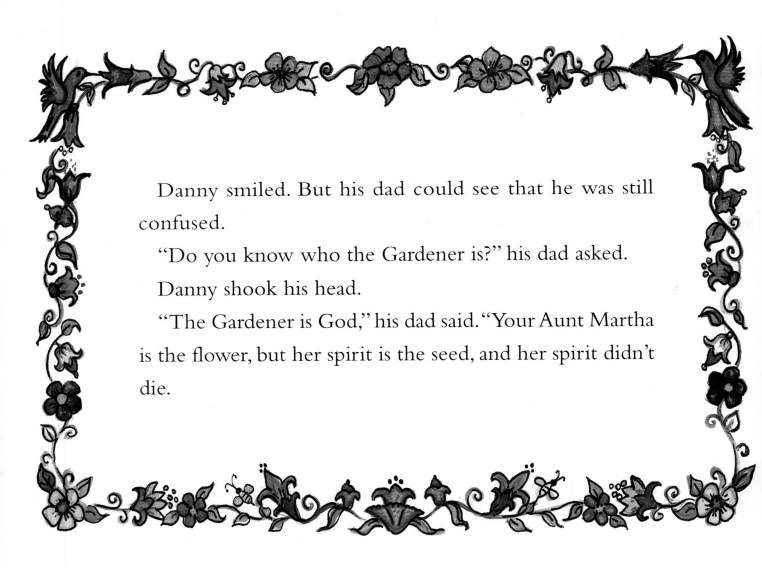

Danny smiled. But his dad could see that he was still confused.

"Do you know who the Gardener is?" his dad asked.

Danny shook his head.

"The Gardener is God," his dad said. "Your Aunt Martha is the flower, but her spirit is the seed, and her spirit didn't die.

She lived here with us in our world, like in a garden, and helped make it a beautiful place.

Now God has taken her spirit to Heaven to be with Jesus."

Danny's face lit up. "Heaven is like the most beautiful garden where flowers never die!"

"That's it," his dad said.

Aunt Martha wasn't really in the casket. That was only her body, like a flower. Her spirit, like the seed, was in a new wonderful place.

We came to church to remember Aunt Martha and to celebrate her spirit because we know that we will see her again in Heaven, in God's Garden.